A Collection of Fents

Poetry by

Roland Rutherford Brown

**Grosvenor House
Publishing Limited**

This book is published by
Grosvenor House Publishing Ltd
Link House
140 The Broadway, Tolworth, Surrey, KT6 7HT.
www.grosvenorhousepublishing.co.uk

A CIP record for this book
is available from the British Library

ISBN 978-1-80381-705-7

For Helen, Colette and Carole
Who always said I should

Note on the Author

Roland Brown is retired and lives with his wife in Derbyshire, he has a grown up family and four grandchildren. Spending many years acting at the Lace Market Theatre in Nottingham, where short productions in between major plays were called "*fents*". A fent in lace manufacture is a remnant or piece. He has borrowed the term for the title of this book.

Contents

Roots

We are grey slate, black coal, earth,
gas and canary song.
We are pick and stone,
sightless ponies,
cage and winding gear.
We are colliery back to backs,
fireside baths the
smell of mutton broth,
simmering on black lead stoves.
Screaming neighbours, and
hungry barefoot bairns.
We are deaths neighbour and
black ribboned colliery bands,
community, comradeship, working men's clubs
and beer.
We are the bowls, the gut,
the wealth providers and the
searing dust filled lungs
faced with slag heap retirement
in cold crisp air.
We are grey slate, black coal, earth.
We are our children's children.

Pit Closures in the North East
A Trilogy

"Gannan Yairm"

We're gannan yairm lads
We're gannan yairm.
The pits closing doon
There's nee maa coal.
There ganna get the black stuff
dug up by a Russian or a Pole
or some bugger else, it doesn't matter who,
all ye need to kna lads
it's the end for me and you

We're gannan yairm lads
Wer'e gannan yairm
to sit by a fire that's burning someone else's coal
while the misses scrimps and saves
to manage on the dole.
So lay down your shovels lads,
take off your hobnail boots
They're closing down wa pit
And no one gives two hoots.

We're gannan yairm lads
We're gannan yairm.
Although we kna there's plenty coal doon here
Enough to last a life time
Never mind a year.
They divn't want to pay wa
so they're telling was a lie
they think it's too expensive
so they're hanging was oot to dry.

We're gannan yairm lads
We're gannan yairm,
It doesn't matter that you grafted
giving your body and soul.
One shift on one shift off
hewing out the coal.
It's not just the job loss, it's the community as well
Thousands on wa oot of work
And told politely, go to hell.

We're ganna yairm lads
We're gannan yairm
But this is not the end of the story as surely time will
tell,
it's just another chapter
in the rocky road to hell.
I'll finish off the story sometime, a'll tell yas when
We may be gannan yairm lads
But we'll be back again.

"Mary's Lament"

He puts on his boots,
He's dressed for work
Bait clenched in a big man's fist
It's as if he canna see that it's not there
As if he's looking through a mist.
The man I married was big and strong
handsome, bright and bonnie
a man who thought the world his oyster,
that used to be my Johnnie

The pits been closed now
Six months or more
and still he gans every day
and stands with his marras, sharing a tab
as if they were waiting for their pay.
This shouldn't happen to men like Johnnie
they've worked hard all their lives,
it's a lonely road to rehabilitation
and its only the few that survives

But it's no good crying over spilt milk.
I'm Mary and this is my lament,
so I've got to be strong and show resolve
and go forward with real intent,
so when I hear the clump of his hobnail boots
and I listen for the back door sneck,
I'll greet him with a smile and a great big hug
and throw my arms aroond his neck.
"Its ganna be aall reet pet"

"Johnnie"

I gan to the pit head every day
I know it's bloody mad,
I dress in the clays that I wore doon the pit
and the boots that I got from me dad.
Ye see it's aboot not kna-in what ta dee
when your worlds chopped from under your feet,
it,s about trying to maintain an equilibrium, I think
that's the word,
it's somewhere to talk and to meet.
There's lads roond here that think the Pits al come
back
and we'll aall be returned to wa jobs,
but I don't think so, the works gone now, but
sometimes it's hard to choke back on your sobs
and be the man your misses thinks ya are,
when you knaa all the time that ya not.
But I've got to dee something, pull me sell together
or I'm just ganna stand here and rot.
I'm lucky, there's men here too auld to work again
Or to make another kind of life,
at least I can gan yairm to a hoose that's warm
and the love and support of the wife.

I Remember

I remember when we talked, you and I
As we walked, you and I,
along the beach, you and I.

How we found comfort stones, you and I
and pressed them in each others hands you and I,
and how you wished and I wished you and I
and I wished and you wished you and I
that the world would be you and I.
As it was then, just, you and I.

Hip-Hop

I thank you for your delightful ode
and for its theme its golfing mode.
I like the story, the way you write
although it gave me quite a fright
to think of mighty bionic me
without a crutch stood on the tee.
A clunk a whirr a crunch a clip
and into action goes my bionic hip.
Club head speed not ever seen
as my ball lands right on the green,
it flew through the air, over the trees
now putting is just like shelling peas
and if by chance or slight of hand
my ball should land in bunker sand
once more into action comes my secret hip
and I'm out of the bunker with a simple chip.
The crowds are gathering to watch me play
as I walk the length of the next fairway.
But now it's the drive across the lake
where many a golfer made a big mistake.
The crowds are swarming several deep
as now I take a quantum leap.
But there's a rumble as the crowd all mutter
"My God he's driving with a putter".
Now I'm coming to the last
The secret of my hip held fast.
But "NO" the secret of my hip is out,
I hear the massive throng all shout
as I walk the yards of the last fairway
they all are shouting
HIP- HIP- HOORAY

Coffee

You used to cycle to my house at lunch time,
I don't know any other woman who would do that.
We would hug, one of those 'frightened you'll disappear' hugs,
Then eat lunch that I had made for you,
sometimes salad, sitting in the garden.
You would tell me all about your morning at work
And we'd talk about our plans, the things we would do.
Then you'd drink your coffee, you liked it hot.
I made it early because I was frightened
it would be to hot to drink,
Worried that I had made it too soon and it would be cold.
Another 'frightened you'll disappear' hug
and I would watch you cycle back down the hill to work

I eat lunch in silence now
Sometimes in the garden if it's not too cold.
But see, the coffee that I made for you is still hot
and just right for drinking.

Ada and Wilf

Ada and Wilf were a couple of very dissimilar proportions
Ada was large and when she stood up
you felt she should issue precautions,
She crossed the room like a plate full of jelly,
and on one occasion her hip moved by itself
and knocked over the telly.
Whilst Wilf was a man of diminutive stature
and in everyday life sort of played Dennis
to her Margaret Thatcher.
As the evening gradually drew to a close
and Wilf started to think
of a nights peaceful repose
Ada rose up and said "I'm going to have a bath."
Wilf feigned sleep as he sat by the fire
with his feet in the hearth.
"I'll call for you to scrub my back"
she said as she squeezed out through the door
and Wilf wished he could fall
through that crack in the floor.
"I'm ready" her voice trilled down the stairs
and Wilf quietly went up
saying his prayers.
At the top he peeped round the bathroom door
And sure enough there was water
All over the floor,
and Ada wedged in the bath
like a blancmange all wobbly and pink
and Wilf just didn't know really
quite what he should think.
She gave him the soap and said
"I'll lean forward a bit,"
well the soap shot out of his hand
and down her left tit

into the water followed by one of Ada's big sighs
as he groped for the soap
between her pink thighs
to be realistic he didn't grope much
because to be honest he was frightened
of what else he might touch.
He started to lather with a slight feeling of revulsion
He felt it was like trying to paint their stone wall
with a coat of emulsion.
There were hillocks , humps and valleys
where for the soap he did hunt
and at one point he wasn't sure
if he was washing her back or her front.
Job finished, he was just about to leave
when she said "I think I'm stuck,
Give us a heave."
Well he pushed and he pulled at lumps of pink blubber
But it went back into place
Like she was made out of rubber.
In desperation he stood on the baths sill
and thought where there's a way
there must be a will.
He put his hands right under her armpits
But with Ada you know
nothing quite fits.
He heaved and he pulled
alas to no avail
Ada was stuck in the bath
just like a beached whale
"One more go" he said
"this time its full throttle"
and Ada popped like a champagne cork
out of a bottle.

Wilf wasn't prepared for the tsunami that followed
he coughed and he spluttered
from all the water he'd swallowed.
The sky is all pink he thought
as he looked through watery eyes
then he realised he was on his back
looking up at Ada's big thighs.
"You think this is over Ada
well it's not, not yet"
Wilf said in a voice he thought
he might just regret
"your release from the bath has taken over an hour
from now on, no bath
you just take a shower".
Ada beamed at his manliness
And started to wobble
Oh my God thought Wilf
now I'm in trouble.

Child of My Morning

Child of my morning
Are you child of my sin?
Such loveliness to behold
Such torment within.
Where are you running
My little smile
Stop and hold hands
Just for a while.

Child of my morning
You know no wrong
Where are you going
Are you my life's song?
Oh beauty, movement, smile
Racked with a spasm.
How well, how able am I
To bridge such a chasm?

Child of my morning
Are we questions or answers?
Spinning through life
Like the spirits of dancers.
Whirling to music
Which to you is just sound.
Turning and flailing
On life's merry-go-round.

Child of my morning.
Can you see none of it matters?
A life that seems useless,
A dream that's in tatters.
Chaos in life form
If viewed from above.
Shattered, but bound
By our own kind of love.

Always Kiss Me Goodnight

When you kiss me goodnight
I feel your soft lips on my cheek,
the warmth of your breath,
the scent of your hair.
Always kiss me goodnight

When you are in your world
and I am locked in mine
and words cannot be said,
remember, and always
kiss me goodnight.

When there is frustration and anger
and the world seems upside down
When I can't help you
because of how I am,
Still, always kiss me goodnight

We will be far apart in time to come
But the stars we see
will be the same stars
so remember, and always,
always kiss me goodnight.

Slipped Time

We met in your café, where you serve breakfasts,
and big mugs of tea.
As I looked up, I saw you looking,
looking, directly at me.
I'm not sure, but I think my heart skipped a beat,
so I diverted my eyes
and started to eat.
Next time, you smiled and we both said "hello"
And then, seemed not to care
that our feelings may show.
You agreed to join me
For a cup of tea and a chat
which we did on my visits,
when you could, after that.
You told me you had been seeing someone
"Is it serious" I said.
"No, he works in an office"
"What's his name"
"He's called Fred"
I knew for both of us it was love at first sight,
but I didn't know how to say it,
to make it come right.
The accident kept me away
for well over a year.
The look on your face
the start of a tear.
"I take it you lost interest"? you suddenly said.
"No, I had an accident,
they thought I was dead".

"I got married, to that guy in the office"
"The one you called Fred"?
You nodded and my stomach
Just turned into lead.
"I had hoped" I started to say,
But time had slipped, like tectonic plates,
and the most we could be,
was platonic mates.

Goodbye in a Coffee Bar

Just like you to say it,
"yes two coffees please"
where there's so much noise
I can hardly hear.
"No nothing to eat"
All these people staring
if I raise my voice in anguish.
"Thank you no, not even a sandwich"
Why couldn't you have said it in the park?
When we were alone , or in the dark.
I might have known there'd be a catch,
And what about Twickenham
And that rugby match.
"No nothing more"
Why did you bother to say you care?
Don't just sit saying nothing.
What about the talk of things we'd share?
I can't stand it in here.
You couldn't even tell me in the car.
Just like you to say it here.
Goodbye in a coffee bar.

Supermarket

Going to the Supermarket
through the automatic door
The trolley that I'm pushing
is crabbing sideways across the floor
It's broken.
Got to get potatoes, carrots, a cauliflower
Haven't got much time
just three quarters of an hour
to fill some five 'p' bags
with the items on this list
and when I've got it done
there's sure to be something that I've missed,
tins of beans, tins of peas, tins of soup,
tins of those spaghetti things the kids like
in the shape of little hoops.
Apples, bananas, and loads of soft fruit too
and those funny vegetables
that smell like something that's sticking to your
shoe.
Rushing, crushing, trolleys in all directions.
I'm looking at the aisle signs
that tell me just what sections
are stacking the goods that I *don't* want,
where are the ones that I *do*
this whole crazy business
is like a human zoo.
A voice over the intercom tells me
there's a special offer on Cadburys Selection
and I suddenly see a friend of mine
who buys off the "Crash Section"

Cornflakes, Weetabix, Sugar Puffs as well.
There's got to be another way
to avoid this shopping hell.
I know I could shop on line
That would save some strife,
Or an even better idea,
I'll just send the wife.

A.M.

Cup and
Saucer,
Coffee,
Spoon

Bowl,
Milk and
Meusli
Grenola
Strewn

Coat and
Paper,
Shout
"I'm off"

Start the
Car and
Cigarette,
Cough.

Sales Drive

Driving down the motorway
doing a hundred and ten,
breaking hard, down through the gears
and now I'm wondering when
the guy behind will get out of the way
to let me change the lane
so that I can get in the fast traffic
and up to speed again.
Now there's road works up ahead,
a breeding ground for cones.
Use the car phone if I'm late
like one of those Yuppy Sloans.
Drum the wheel, why don't they move?
The tail-back's several miles,
the heater in the seat is too hot
probably give me piles.
What's that pratt doing nudging in?
I'll just close the space,
that got him! Stupid berk.
Just look at his tensed up face.
Really some of these people
Just don't know how to drive,
So impatient and all stressed up
They're lucky to be alive.
Ah! here we go, we're off again
Nicely picking up speed.
Up on his inside, cross over in front
gobble the miles in greed.
This is the junction, No! Yes it is!
I'll still be on time I bet.
It isn't that hot, I wonder what's wrong
I seem to be covered in sweat.
Just round this corner, here it is.

I knew I'd hardly be late.
The journey down? No problem at all
In fact it was really great.
What do you mean sit down relax?
I am relaxed you can see
You're sorry about the order!
Because you can't place it with me......

We Shall Remember Them

We shall remember them.
We don't remember him, father's brother,
who died at Passchendaele or Ypres,
or was it on the Somme.
We don't remember him,
his memories are gone.

We shall remember those
who died in poppy fields of red.
We don't remember him
Fathers brother – Ned?

We shall remember them
with symbolic pomp and joy.
Yet we don't remember him
who died alone,
Grandmother's boy.

Unknown Soldiers

I didn't see trench warfare
or the bloody blown off limbs.
I didn't see the bodies
or hear comrades whispered hymns.
I didn't see the carnage,
uniforms red with blood
or try to join the advance
through life sapping mud.
I didn't have to shoot my wounded horse
sometime my only friend
or lie in filthy slime
my life to chance depend.
I didn't breath mustard gas
or get shell shock, as they called it then,
or give or receive the order to "go over"
time and time again.
I didn't see trench warfare
or hold some mothers dying son.
I didn't see trench warfare, but I am, I am
because they did each and every one.

Song
We're going over the top boys
We're going over the top
"Gawd Almighty" we'll be in Blighty
Then down to the pub we'll pop

We're going over the top boys
We're going over the top
We've got the Hun on the run
Soon this bloody war will stop

We're going over the top boys
We're going over the top
We're out of the trench, free of the stench
Now we are running the shop

We're going over the top boys
We're going over the top
Guns ablaze, I can't see through this haze
I've bought it so...now my song.....must...stop.

Life's Love

You could not look more fair, than as now I see you
Walking down a country lane, skirt swaying with the
movement of your hips,
The breeze giving wispy movements to your hair,
and unspent kisses budding on your lips.

There is nothing now with which I can compare your
beauty.
Your eyes, your smile, your face
that gives to you not mere tranquillity
But a gentle grace.

And if the observer sees you, as one to whom
age has been no kinder than to the rest
with skin that shows the signs of time and sun
and where the cloak of troubles past its marks invest

Then I am blind,
for I see you now as before
Unchanged by the seasons
and with a beauty that takes no heed of natures law.

Morecambe in November

From the rain splashed hotel window,
the November sea, a flat grey sheet,
merges with the beach like the tonal shade
of a black and white photograph.
Blue-black clouds, occasionally polka dotted
with the whiteness of gulls, scudding in the wind.
Whilst wellington boots and anoraks
Walk oblivious dogs.

Seafront Villa Hotels, the Polydor and Sea View,
yesterdays boarding houses, still with faded blinds,
crowd the promenade and dare the encroaching sea,
like foot soldiers awaiting the advance.
The shining wet empty street
splashed with the red of a moving raincoat
signals the retreat of another season.
Rows of hanging unlit bulbs.
Frontierland , Ghost Town of the West.
And blank neon amusement arcades with Pin Ball
and One Armed Bandits in a state of oily rest.

Dropping the curtain, you hear the chink of coin
that conjures up the harvest of that other town.
With flashing lights, fish and chips,
kiss-me-quick and helter-skelter.
Ice Cream, Candy Floss,
and gun fights at the not so O.K. Coraal.
Throbbing, pulsating, disco dancing,
bubbling pan of broth.
Turned off with the power cut of seasons end.

Love Unanswered A Trilogy

Tomorrow

I stand at the window, watching the grey damp
day gradually unfold

Thinking, thinking of you, remembering and missing you

Remembering that we *have* stood on a mountain,
bathed in the sea

and soared higher than an eagle, spinning,
spinning in ecstasy

and scattering our dreams like dandelion
clocks on the winds of tomorrow.

But there is no tomorrow, only today and we live with
our memories of yesterday,

It's never enough,

I remember what you say, that we must be
thankful for what we have

and I am, but it is still not enough

Who knows, maybe, just maybe, there will
be a tomorrow for us.

Dilemma

I turn the page
It's the end of the chapter.
The end of the chapter
but not the end of the story.
An all too familiar tale of,
"they cannot be together
but they cannot be apart."
I put down the book
afraid to read on
and watch the early evening dappled sunlight
seemingly seep into the pages.
So many hills climbed,
so many valleys descended
so many rushing rivers
and calm gently flowing streams
of peace and love.
Head or heart,
Head or heart
Only time can intervene.
But I have to know.
I pick up the book and start to read.

Acceptance

Now the book is returned to the shelf.
Their Summer drifts into the Autumn of their lives
with no resolve.
Memories of summers joy, laughter,
love, peace and the knowledge that things will not,
cannot change .
But grateful for what they have
and what they've had.
Just an unspoken acceptance

Dark Waters

I wept for you deep in my soul,
where the rocks are and the pain is.
Where there's darkness and the places I can't go.
Where dark waters run,
and I here your child's voice,
feel your child's hand, remember,
and burn with my memories fire.
I drink from your cup of acceptance
Sleep in the cradle of your heart.
Salt tears, and the wind moaning through the
trees of my soul

Togetherness

She gave him cycle clips for Christmas
He gave her long knickers with elastic in the legs.
She sat reading on the sofa.
He watched television.
They shared a walk and corned beef sandwiches on
Boxing Day
His favourites, she thought.
He wanted cheese.

They talked of – his friends – her friends – their
friends Bob and Mary
He sort of liked Bob but not Mary
She didn't sort of like either of them,
but then neither did he.
They went on holiday with them every year and
for a drink with them every week.

He kissed her goodnight as she slid into bed next to
him
She looked young and lovely
"Thank you for a nice Christmas dear", they said
as the light went out.
I can't ride a bike, he thought
She thought, I only wear briefs or a thong.
They shared sleep

1.5 Degrees C

1.5 degrees C, can we attain it?
Or get below,
Of course its possible the scientists know
1.5 degrees C

We already have melting snow caps
and glacial reduction
twenty eight million tons, between
1994 and 2017
1.5 degrees C

If we attain it we still face drought,
famine and entire ecosystems wiped out
with 100 million in poverty just
because we aren't acting as quick as we must
1.5 Degrees C

Attribution Science covers a range
to tell us how much of disasters
are due to Climate Change
1.5 Degrees C

Hurricane Harvey in 2017 cost 90 billion dollars flat
Climate Change was 67 billion of that
El Nino 2.5 billion trees perished too
Emitting 49.5 million tons of CO_2
1.5 degrees C

So as individuals what can we do?
What you can afford it's down to you
Solar Panels, Hybrid and Electric Cars
All can be cheaper than getting to Mars
1.5 Degrees C

Recycling by us is making a start
But we need governments to play a much bigger part
Wake up it's our planet we are destroying
Don't wait until all we have is a memory
to which we are cloying
1.5 Degrees C.

Remembrance

Now I gather flowers in remembrance,
and fill my world with their transient beauty
a tableau to you.
When they wither and die,
Lying where they fall,
I shall not weep.
They are but a token of that which is
not of face or flesh,
not of touch nor sound,
but of spirit.

Now the mansions that I did not build for you
remain in rubble.
To grow in soaring marble columns
only in the mind.
An edifice to what was or might have been.
And when they too fall
with the tiredness of old dreams,
I must not despair, nor give way to grief,
nor languish in self pity,
but remember your purity.

Now the portraits of my youth
hanging in the lofty halls of experience
must be cloaked in dust,
no longer open to your naked stare.
The sallow skinned, grimy boy,
who's limbs grew in supple strength for you,
returned in broken frame
to the attics of the mind.
Leaving cobweb trails in thoughts
of love for you.

Now I gather flowers in remembrance,
flowers reaching up in the waving corn,
unfettered by time or ritual.
Red with blood, blue with sky,
reflections of your freedom.
Transcending that which is,
but can never be.
That which seemed short lived,
but lives on and is eternal

The Annex

I went to Anne Franks house today,
no one there,
I climbed steep staircases
and went into rooms bare
and unwelcoming.
Through the bookcase door
hearing the sound of jackboots
scraping on the floor.
Shared the intimacy of film star pictures
pasted with a corner curl
on brown papered walls
hung by a dreaming girl.

The family room, behind closed doors,
full of silent whispered fears
gathering like cobwebs in the corners
of those two long years.
Heard the knock and "open up"
And then the voices say
"Ja ich bien ein Juden"
and then softly drift away.
The sun shone in Prinsengracht,
a breeze ruffled through my hair.
I stood a moment, then strolled away
smelling blossom in the air.

Love Light

Dark clouds conspire with nightfall
to make the darkness complete.
Moon through the labyrinth
dapples water with light,
and fish see to swim.
One by one you sketch my stars,
like switching on tiny lights,
showing me your way
through my darkness.
Until you dissolve with
swirling morning mists
and I am left
with dampness,
dimpled pillow,
cold bed.
Awaiting nights darkness.

Lo demas era muerte
y solo muerte a las
cinco de la tarde

(The rest was death
and death alone
at five in the afternoon)

Federico Garcia Lorca

No Bulls Died That Sunday Afternoon

No bulls died that Sunday afternoon
Heat caked sweat on his body
The searing pain of voices heard, blinded.
Only the ripping of gut
and internal bleeding
When will it stop,
The twisting, churning, rending apart.
The impossible, become possible
The impregnable penetrated.
Cut down like ripening corn.
Discarding the innards
of sacredness like so much offal.
Left flailing like a bloody rag
On the horn of infidelity.
They cannot see the bleeding,
Wrapped in the cape of challenge.
The sky was blue, the heat shimmered in the dust,
But strangely
No bulls died, that Sunday afternoon

Redundant

I signed on at the DSS
among faceless men
of no address.
Standing in the mumbling queue
of those who'd done it
and knew just who
they ought to see
to make their claim,
for another week
with a jobless aim

"You understand we can't help you,
you're management"
It's like standing in a human zoo
"You'd probably do better by yourself,
but face up to it Mr. Er...
you're on the shelf.
At your age
we know from extrapolation
It isn't even worthwhile
completing an application".
"Sign on again two weeks from now"
said the smiling face
that I called cow.
Not to her face, goes without saying
But she made me feel
I was reduced to praying
for someone to say
Don't worry, you're not to blame
We know it's the recession that put out the flame.

Two hundred applications dead
and the postman calling
still gets me out of bed.
A management club for exec's
that can't raise a penny
from their local TECs,
to make a start with their own venture
But, I'm told I'm well rounded with another dimension
So I'll just use that
And bugger the pension.

Coming Through The Day

The curtain of iron black night
and all its silent, innermost, deep most, fear most thoughts,
rises to the creeping light of dawn and its chorus.
Setting the stage for another, hurry by, scurry by,
no time to talk by day.
The cast, gathering in the street, walking, bussing,
riding down the milk bottle chinking road that leads
to work, to play, to mum, to school, to the park bench
and picking breakfast from the waste bin on the way.

We step now on to this our stage
and stride the boards of day, footlights, arcs, spots, lighting us.
as now we stand centre stage and deliver unrehearsed lines
and tremble with our private thoughts and fears,
beneath the white tight , pancake mask, which is all they see,
the other actors, audience, fellow players in our scene.
Pay attention ! lest we forget our words!
Don't cry! just lie! don't scream!
For this, is a happy scene.

We bumble, jumble, tumble through the day.
The chorus of voices, the silence of libraries.
The rushing, hooting, exhaust smelling traffic of our street.
In dream-like sequence one and then another of those
who played our part before us
step from the shadows of our stage
and give us arm wrapped shoulders.
As now with confidence we step our way
Through the black-blue, grey-blue, blue-blue day

The curtain of iron-black night,
snow-soft, paper-light, dust-like, closes on the day,
as each player now takes their bow at curtains call
and we still hear applause amid the thunder of nights silence.
For we who crept with fear to centre stage, have come through
the day and look out now at warm lit windows reflecting
rain splashed, people dashed, lamp lit streets.
That wend their way to, nowhere, somewhere? Everywhere
that makes the scene, that starts tomorrows play.

Face

What do you see, if you look
beyond the rheumy eyes, the slackened mouth
the skin that's like the leather binding of some old book
that holds the secrets of a life.
A boy, a youth, a man who loved and lost
and loved again and found a wife.
Of times spent walking barefoot on the sand
with a little girl beside you
who held tightly to your hand.
The hands of time move swiftly
its morning as they sweep past noon
now its evening and you start to see
the shadows of the moon
The lines of joy and sorrow
etched on parchment with no grace
that now look back towards you.
The story, that is your face.

Langley Mill

Langley Mill, name appealing like church bells on Sunday morn.
But alas, most deceiving for a place quite so forlorn.
Station Road, with chip and curry papers blowing in the
evening breeze wrapping round the drunken youth who is
crawling on his knees, declaring love that is undying to his girl
who puffs her fag
and who, in a colloquialism would be called something not
much nicer than a slag.
Boarded shops, peeling plaster, faded past of mine and mill,
Under the railway bridge and by St Andrews
And geranium pots on window sills

Now the sound of leather on willow and the chink of cricket
teas,
Close the eyes and in a another place
This would be a scene to please.
Instead we have a boundary fence telling us "Kilroy was here"
Scribed in psycadelic spray paint
by unknown artist, of no particular career.
But progress comes to Langley Mill as buildings start to be
pulled down
Roofs and chimneys, walls and windows
Is this the end of this little town?

Away with the Chinese Takeaway and the local garage too.
What will fill the space created?
Someone said it will be a zoo
But supermarket is the bye word, there are only three nearby
So Sainsbury's or Waitrose
could be built to block out the sky.
But we learn the cry is Asda, the local council have done a deal
and Langley Mill the shopping centre
ends up in Wall Marts fishing creel.

Moth Balls

I pissed on a moth,
in the urinal, off the public bar
of the Old Swan Hotel.
It flew through the window
attracted by light and white
porcelain. Flying kamikaze like
into a Niagara of recycled Worthington E.
Splashed against the cold white slab
of instant, one hundred percent morgue -
ages I watched it float on the yellow river.
Like an unlit Viking funeral pyre,
heading for some plug hole Valhalla,
Life like a candle.
"Two pints of Worthington please landlord"

Referendum

Lower the Saltire,
Raise up the Jack
The people have spoken
there's no turning back.
Sound the knell
from Glasgow to Aberdeen,
the voices have been heard
it's the end of a dream.
Magnanimous in victory.
Noble in defeat,
no glory to trumpet,
no drum to be beat.
A country divided
must once more join hands
for better or worse
the Union stands.

Old Age

You stand at your netted window
Dim eyes peering out, to a world
no longer known to you.
Back stooped like some colossus
erected to life's burden.

Flesh hangs grey and useless
Where once muscle moved you
in an easy sinuous way.
Now you shuffle from the window
to your sodden bed

Grease stains the dressing gown held with
trembling hand
as childlike you dribble time away,
between the meals that come,
living for the voice they bring,
dying with the closing door.

Moments when senility fades away
Come thoughts which bring a tear
for memories of touch and company.
For shame at peeling papered walls
and degradation, your total loss of dignity

You stand at your netted window.
Who smiles? Who sees your emptiness
or hears your silence when you cry,
who comforts your crumbling decay?
When I am you, I think I'll want to die.

Ode To A Bacon Roll

Ye know the chieftain o' the pudding race,
well no man's platter would you disgrace.
A crusty roll with floury bloom
and bacon rashers to fill your room,
while butter oozes ore your lips
then down the munchers chin it drips.
Rack o' lamb or fillet steak,
Rich man's food or poor man's cake,
fit for a king or lowly man,
the smell, the juices from the pan
would cause them all to salivate
for a bacon roll set on their plate.
Bacon smoked or bacon plain
to feed the man or feed the wain.
Bacons your man, the roll the wife
In time of plenty or time of strife.
So if for food ye feel forsaken
remember the mighty roll and bacon.

I Heard The Owl Call My Name

The winds blew,
Snow formed the hills into downy white breasts.
The sky was shot with ice blue and gold
as the sun set,
and wild geese flew in chevron to a warmer land.
The stag paused one foot raised, listening,
before entering the darkened forest.
The hare curled for warmth in the undergrowth
All was still
And I heard the Owl call my name.